Defense Reforms

The FY 2017 National Defense Authorization Act included the most sweeping reforms since the Goldwater-Nichols Department of Defense Reorganization Act of 1986.

Do you support these reforms?

I am familiarizing myself with the extensive reforms enacted by this legislation, and will evaluate their impact on organizations, processes, and people once I get a handle on them. These reforms deserve my full attention and if confirmed I will comply with the law and also provide the Congress with the assessments it requires and any suggestions for change that seem appropriate.

What other areas for defense reform do you believe might be appropriate for this Committee to address?

At this time, I have no additional areas to recommend. If confirmed, I will look carefully at any other areas.

Duties of the Secretary of Defense

Section 113 of title 10, United States Code, provides that the Secretary of Defense is the principal assistant to the President in all matters relating to the Department of Defense. Subject to the direction of the President, the Secretary of Defense, under section 113, has authority, direction, and control over the Department of Defense (DOD).

Do you believe there are actions you need to take to enhance your ability to perform the duties of the Secretary of Defense?

Current authorities for the Secretary of Defense are sufficient.

What changes to section 113, if any, would you recommend?

I have no recommendations at this time. If confirmed, and once in office, I will keep the Committee advised if my views change.

You retired from the United States Marine Corps on June 1, 2013. For the President to appoint you as Secretary of Defense it would require Congress to pass legislation to provide an exception to the requirement that a Secretary of Defense must have been relieved from active status for a period of seven years.

What qualities, qualifications and characteristics would you bring to the position of Secretary of Defense, if confirmed, that would warrant an exception to this 7 year requirement of section 113?

I defer to the Congress regarding whether or not an exception is warranted. Having demonstrated 40 years of loyalty to the principle of civilian control and to the U.S. Constitution, I know what to expect from the uniformed leadership in their interactions with the Department's civilian leaders. Furthermore, I understand what is required of the civilians tasked with leading our military services.

If such legislation is enacted, and if confirmed, how would you ensure that your tenure as Secretary of Defense reflects the requirement for civilian control of the Armed Forces that is embodied in our Constitution as implemented in section 113?

If confirmed as the Department's civilian leader, I will put the right team in place to provide civilian leadership across the Department of Defense, ensure feedback loops are robust, and be responsive to the Congress.

Priorities

If confirmed, you will confront a range of critical issues relating to threats to national security and ensuring that the Armed Forces are prepared to deal with these threats.

In your view, what are the major challenges confronting the next Secretary of Defense?

Globally we face a world awash in change. Adapting our security posture to emerging threats will be a continuing effort in the Department. Internal to our processes, the major challenge is to determine, request, and allocate the resources necessary to strengthen our military, while earning the confidence of the Congress and the American people that the Department of Defense is a good steward of taxpayer money. Externally, the major challenges include nation states choosing to be strategic competitors, like Russia and China; other nations that are supporting terrorist groups or violating non-proliferation protocols; and the ongoing threat posed by terrorist groups like ISIS.

Assuming you are confirmed, what plans do you have for addressing these challenges?

My obligation would be to convey to the President and the Committee the risks we face as a nation due to the changing nature of these external threats and the internal constraints posed by the Budget Control Act sequester. My immediate aim would be to balance the competing demands of carrying out the strategic objectives established by the President, while resetting our force. We must strengthen our military in order to adapt to changing threats. We must also take no ally for granted, and the Department of Defense, should I be confirmed, will work to promote these alliances, operating in alignment with the Department of State.

If confirmed, what broad priorities would you establish in terms of issues which must be addressed by the Secretary of Defense?

My priorities would include increasing the readiness of our force, and ensuring its effective employment in accomplishing the missions directed by the Commander-in-Chief. I intend to bring business-minded reforms to the Department of Defense, ensuring that we gain the greatest possible return to our national security for every tax dollar invested. This effort would include a review of what, why, and how we are buying things.

Chain of Command

Section 162(b) of title 10, United States Code, provides that the chain of command runs from the President to the Secretary of Defense and from the Secretary of Defense to the combatant commands. Section 163(a) of title 10 further provides that the President may direct communications to combatant commanders through the Chairman of the Joint Chiefs of Staff and may assign duties to the Chairman to assist the President and the Secretary of Defense in performing their command function.

Do you believe that these provisions facilitate a clear and effective chain of command?

Having seen these provisions in practice, I believe they are clear and effective.

In your view, do these provisions enhance or degrade civilian control of the military?

I believe these provisions enhance civilian control.

Are there circumstances in which you believe it is appropriate for U.S. military forces to be under the operational command or control of an authority outside the chain of command established under title 10, United States Code?

There are times when tactical and operational considerations dictate that military capabilities be made temporarily available to support an activity of the government other than the Department of Defense. It can be appropriate under such circumstances that the head of another department or agency direct operations while working with the Secretary of Defense. At all times, the Commander-in-Chief remains at the top of our chain of command, and the U.S. military operates under U.S. control. Further, U.S. military personnel remain at all times subject to the Uniform Code of Military Justice.

Advice of the Chairman of the Joint Chiefs of Staff

Section 151 of title 10, United States Code, provides, in part, that the Chairman of the Joint Chiefs of Staff is the principal military adviser to the President, the National Security Council, and the Secretary of Defense.

In your view, how will your status as a recently retired general officer impact this statutory relationship between the Chairman of the Joint Chiefs of Staff and the Secretary of Defense?

Like all American commissioned officers, I was taught to respect the concept of civilian control of the military from my first day in uniform. I forecast no impact from my past service.

The Joint Chiefs and the Combatant Commanders

Section 921 of the FY17 NDAA made changes to section 151 of title 10, United States Code, concerning the functions of the Joint Chiefs of Staff.

What is your assessment of the authorities for providing uniformed professional military judgment, advice, and opinions to the President, National Security Council, and civilian leadership of the Department of Defense?

I believe that the authorities are appropriate. If confirmed, I will notify this committee if I change my assessment while in office.

What changes in law, if any, do you think may be necessary to ensure that the views of the Service Chiefs and of the combatant commanders are presented and considered?

At this time, I do not see the need for any change in the law.

Joint Force Headquarters and Component Commands

Does the current model for creating joint force headquarters below the unified command level meet the needs of modern warfare and the global challenges we face?

Yes.

In your view, would the combatant commands' contingency planning and preparedness be improved by creating subordinate joint force headquarters prior to crises?

If confirmed, I will look carefully at the ability of combatant commanders to create such headquarters.

1What are the chief obstacles to establishing such headquarters and what could be done to overcome them?

Other than manpower constraints for staffing additional headquarters, I am unaware of obstacles. If confirmed, I will examine this issue and advise the committee should we find obstacles.

Use of Military Force

In your view, what factors should be considered in making recommendations to the President on the use of military force?

If confirmed, the factors that I will consider include the nature of the threat to our vital interests, whether non-military methods are sufficient to address the threat, whether such methods have been exhausted, and the importance of a defined and militarily achievable political end state.

In your view, what is the appropriate role of the Secretary of Defense in establishing policies for the use of military force, and rules of engagement? What is the appropriate role of the combatant commanders?

The appropriate role of the Secretary of Defense is to engage in the formulation of policy; to ensure the political end state is defined; to ensure a whole-of-government approach, integrating diplomatic, economic, and military efforts; to give clear guidance to our military for its operational role and its rules of engagement; and to maintain a dialogue with Combatant Commanders, who provide recommendations on the above as well as recommended courses of action.

Do you agree with the Obama administration's interpretation of the 2001 Authorization for the Use of Military Force (AUMF)?

In the absence of Congressional action to provide a new or revised AUMF, I believe the enemy threat was sufficiently compelling for the current administration to use the 2001 version.

Is the 2001 AUMF sufficient authorization for the military operations being conducted against ISIS?

I will review the 2001 AUMF with the Chairman of the Joint Chiefs of Staff if I am confirmed and advise the Congress on my conclusions.

National Security Budget Reductions

The original discretionary caps imposed by the Budget Control Act (BCA) will be in effect for FY 2018 through FY 2021, unless there is agreement to change budget

levels.

> **In your assessment, what would be the impacts of continued implementation of the BCA discretionary caps through 2021 on the Department of Defense and national security?**

The impacts would be a weakened military and the need to recalibrate our ability to assert U.S. influence across the world. We have a strategic mismatch between the political ends we espouse and the military means we have available to confront and deter threats. While our military remains the best fighting force in the world, these cuts have created damage that will take time to repair. Unless the Department of Defense receives funds above the caps imposed by the Budget Control Act, it will not be able to achieve the readiness, modernization, and force structure required to meet emerging threats.

> **You, and previous Secretaries of Defense, have expressed concern that underfunding of non-Department of Defense departments and agencies, including the State Department, can have a negative impact on U.S. national security. As was the case in both Bipartisan Budget Act 2013 and 2015, the increases above BCA were equivalent for both defense and non-defense.**

> **Do you believe that any future budget agreements must maintain that dollar-for-dollar principle?**

No. While the solvency and security of the U.S. go hand-in-hand, I believe budgets should match resources to national priorities. Each department and agency must define and justify its requirements. I also believe that all elements of national power must work in tandem to support national priorities—in particular, our diplomatic efforts must be sufficiently funded if we wish the military to be employed generally as a last resort. A process that imposes budget rules first, and matches resources to national priorities second, is inherently limiting and inflexible.

> **If confirmed, by what standards would you measure the adequacy of DOD funding?**

I would measure the adequacy of the Department of Defense's funding by our ability to execute our chosen strategy, maintain the nation's technological edge, preserve the health of the joint force, and provide options to the President. As part of the framework to measure the sufficiency of our resourcing I would also revisit with the Chairman the way we assess, discuss, measure, and convey risk—a process that is fundamental to informing our recommendations regarding the adequacy of funding.

Readiness of the Armed Forces

> **How would you assess the current state of readiness?**

The United States Armed Forces are the finest in the world, but there is no room for complacency. Although I have been a private citizen for over three years, and have not been receiving classified briefings, my understanding is that the current and future readiness of the force could be significantly improved. If confirmed, once I am in office I will get a better handle on this issue.

How would you plan to restore full spectrum readiness and under what timeline? Additionally, how would you enforce those timelines to ensure that goals are met?

If confirmed, among my first priorities in office will be to work with the President and the Congress on a budget that accelerates restoration of full spectrum readiness, ensuring that our military's size and composition are adequate to the tasks at hand. Prior to confirmation, I am unable to provide a detailed timeline. If confirmed, I will work closely with our military and civilian leaders in the Pentagon and with the Congress to establish these accelerated timelines and hold people accountable to meeting them. I assure the Committee that I will be guided by the principle that the military must look at every week as its last week of peace if it is going to be sufficiently prepared for the unexpected.

DOD Financial Management

The Defense Department is the only federal agency that cannot present auditable financial statements showing where and how it spends its annual budget. It also been at high risk for waste, fraud, abuse, and mismanagement by the Comptroller General. Despite much effort and billions spent to fix these problems, they have remained for decades.

What actions will you take or direct that will achieve a better outcome than past actions and initiatives for financial auditability of the Defense Department?

I support the goal of Department of Defense audit readiness. I am keenly aware of the issue and have reviewed key assessments and recommendations from the Government Accountability Office. If confirmed, I will personally and fully review past and ongoing efforts in order to find out what has thwarted out ability to sustain audits. Having defined the problem, I will then direct corrective action, and also which courses of action—with associated timelines and resourcing requirements—we should prioritize to reach auditability in the shortest feasible timeframe.

Department of Defense and Department of Veterans Affairs Collaboration

The Departments of Defense and Veterans Affairs have in recent years increased collaboration to support servicemembers as they transition to veteran status. This support includes access to medical and mental health care services, improved disability evaluation processes, and coordination of compensation and other benefits.

If confirmed, what would you do to ensure that the Department of Defense and Veterans Affairs fully cooperate with each other to streamline processes further to achieve more seamless transition as servicemembers move to veteran status?

I support better integration and cooperation between the Departments of Defense and Veterans Affairs to ensure that our troops receive proper care from both organizations during the hand-off from the DoD to the VA. If confirmed, I will make it among my top priorities to improve the seamlessness of the transition for service members, and will assess issues including the standardization of separation processes and the efficient transfer of service members' records to the Department of Veterans Affairs at the end of active service. I will work closely with all concerned committees on this important issue.

Integrated Disability Evaluation System

The Integrated Disability Evaluation System (IDES) integrates the DOD and Department of Veterans Affairs (VA) disability systems to improve and expedite processing of service members through the disability evaluation system.

What is your assessment of the need to further streamline and improve the IDES?

Our nation has an obligation to ensure that those who have served receive any care that they may need. In the past, the linkage between the military and the Department of Veterans Affairs has not always been effective. I am not yet sufficiently well-informed on the details of the Integrated Disability Evaluation System to provide the thoughtful answer this question deserves but, if confirmed, I will work to ensure that we exceed expectations on all matters under the Department of Defense's control, and collaborate with the Department of Veterans Affairs to ensure an effective hand-off from the DoD to the VA.

If confirmed, how would you work with the VA Secretary to ensure both DOD and VA continually exceed timeliness goals through each phase of the multi-step disability evaluation process?

If confirmed, I will work with the Secretary of Veterans Affairs to change any process that fails to meet transitioning service members' needs or timeliness goals. I will also examine ways to innovate and employ the use of new technologies that could provide for more seamless transitions.

Sexual Assault Prevention and Response

What is your view of the adequacy of the training and resources the Services have in place to investigate and respond to allegations of sexual assault?

Sexual assault violates the core values of the military and must never be tolerated. The Department recognizes that sexual assault is a crime and that criminal behavior in the military is unacceptable. The Department must always strive to eliminate criminal behavior in the ranks and reduce sexual assault incidents to zero. It is clear the Department has a long way to go to fix this problem. If confirmed, I will examine the adequacy of the training and resources currently available, and I will work with the Congress to address this or any problem that affects the readiness of the force.

What is your assessment of the potential impact, if any, of proposals to remove the disposition authority from military commanders over violations of the Uniform Code of Military Justice, including sexual assaults?

If I am confirmed I will take proactive steps to ensure the Services hold leaders accountable at all levels of the military chain of command for carrying out their responsibilities to investigate and adjudicate any potential violations of the Uniform Code of Military Justice. At the present time, I oppose removing disposition authority from military commanders for any criminal behavior in their units. The Department will continue to hold commanders responsible for ensuring the protection of the troops under their command and for ensuring the good order and discipline of their units. Removing disposition authority from commanders would relieve them of these solemn responsibilities and it would ultimately make the problem worse, not better. It would undermine the ability of the military chain of command to ensure that sexual assault allegations are investigated and adjudicated consistent with the rules and regulations of the Uniformed Code of Military Justice.

What is your assessment of the military's protections against retaliation for reporting sexual assault?

The military's protections against retaliation are not completely effective or sufficient. The Department must do more to ensure service members can report any crime, including a crime involving sexual assault, without fear of retaliation. I understand that last year the Department of Defense developed a Retaliation Prevention and Response Strategy aimed at addressing allegations of retaliatory conduct resulting from the reporting of a sexual assault or sexual harassment. If confirmed, I intend to examine the early implementation of that strategy and assess whether further improvements are needed. I also intend to work with the Inspector General and the Military Services to ensure that our approach to reducing and preventing retaliation is effective.

Role of National Guard and Reserves

As the Active Forces have been drawn down, the Reserve Components have been mobilized more in order for the military to meet the requirements of the National Military Strategy.

In your view, what is the appropriate relationship between the Active Forces and

the Reserve Components?

I have personally witnessed the valor and skillfulness of service members in our Reserve Components, honed by more than a decade of combat side-by-side with the Active Force. It is my view that the total force approach to active duty, Guard, and reserve personnel has worked well for decades, and that elements of the Reserve Components must serve as our operational and strategic reserves.

In your view, do the Reserve Components serve as an operational reserve, a strategic reserve, or both? Which role should they occupy going forward?

With smaller Active Forces and a challenging security environment, elements of the Reserve Components must serve as both an operational reserve and strategic reserve.

If Active Duty end strength is increased, what specific parameters would you use to most appropriately determine what a corresponding Reserve Component end strength should be set at in order to support those Active Duty forces?

If confirmed, I would approach the active-reserve mix from a total force perspective with two goals in mind: First, to ensure that larger Active Forces have the reserve enablers required to meet their mission; second, to ensure that the Reserve Components have ample combat capability to complement or reinforce the Active Force in the event of sustained ground combat.

Women in the Military

In December 2015, Secretary Carter changed assignment policy for women in military service, opening all occupations and units to them, including ground combat units in the Army and Marine Corps.

Are you satisfied that the decision to open combat arms units and positions to women was based on an adequate review of the analysis conducted by the military services?

I believe that Secretary Carter appropriately carried out his duties. I have not personally reviewed the data and analysis that Secretary Carter had available to him before he made a decision on this issue. For that reason, I cannot characterize whether the review was adequate.

Do you believe that the occupational standards developed by the military services, especially those developed for the ground combat occupations, reflect "actual, regular, and recurring duties" of the occupation in question, as required by law?

If confirmed, I will study the rationale and implementation of occupational standards across each of the Services. I will regularly consult with the Committee on the basis for occupational standards.

Selective Service Act

Do you believe the Selective Service system, with its focus on supplying large numbers of replacement combat soldiers, meets the needs of today's military and the type of personnel that would likely need to be drafted in a future conflict, including skilled personnel in the medical, linguistic, cyber, and other specialist fields? If not, what changes would you recommend to the Selective Service System?

If confirmed, I will direct the Department of Defense to determine which needed skills are anticipated and pass these requirements to the Selective Service.

Costs of Medical Care

According to the Congressional Budget Office, DOD requested $47 billion in operation and support funding for the military health system in 2016, about 9 percent of the total funding requested for the Department's base budget. CBO has calculated that those costs will reach $64 billion by 2030 if their growth reflects anticipated national trends in health care costs.

What is your assessment of the long-term impact of the Department's health care costs on military readiness and overall national security?

When internal costs rise faster than the topline growth, the Department will be forced to shortchange warfighting. In the nation at large, the rising cost of healthcare continues to outpace inflation by double digits. The same math applies to the Department of Defense, where efforts to improve outcomes while lowering costs have fallen short of expectations.

If confirmed, what actions would you take to mitigate the effect of the Department's rising medical costs on DOD's budget top-line while simultaneously implementing programs to improve health outcomes and to enhance the experience of care for all beneficiaries?

This is a complex issue. If confirmed, I will study it with the guidance of the Committee, taking into account the important reforms included in the National Defense Authorization Act of 2017.

Defense Health Agency

Section 702 of the National Defense Authorization Act for Fiscal Year 2017 transferred oversight and management of military hospitals and clinics from the military services to the Defense Health Agency (DHA).

If confirmed, how would you ensure a rapid and efficient transfer of the operations of those medical facilities to the DHA?

If confirmed, I will assess this issue and keep the Committee informed as the Department works to implement the law rapidly and efficiently.

If confirmed, how would you ensure that the military services reduce their medical headquarters staffs and infrastructure to reflect the changing scope and size of their missions?

Headquarters staff structure should be based on an assessment of the manpower needed to accomplish assigned tasks. I take a similar view of infrastructure requirements, while understanding that superior health outcomes for service members and their families must remain the most important metric for success. Removing redundancy in various headquarters is an opportunity to find savings.

Health Care Quality and Access to Care in the Military Health System (MHS)

If confirmed, what actions would you take with respect to each of the following:

Eliminating performance variability throughout the MHS.

I have witnessed many fine deeds performed by the Military Health System in support of the fighting force over the past 15 years of combat. I am also aware that reviews of the system have identified performance variability issues, and I know that additional direction on this matter is included in the National Defense Authorization Act for Fiscal Year 2017. The Department must improve its ability to establish common performance measures. I understand the Department has reported to Congress on its efforts to date, and, if confirmed, I will make it a priority to oversee implementation of improvements in this area.

Improving health outcomes of the Department's beneficiaries in the direct and purchased care components of the MHS.

I am aware of new direction in the National Defense Authorization Act for Fiscal Year 2017 regarding health outcome measures and improvements. If confirmed, I will ensure accountability for leaders on this issue.

Delivering quality health care at lower cost to create value for beneficiaries and the Department.

This is a major challenge for the American health care system as a whole, including the Military Health System. The system needs to implement business reforms, eliminate redundancy, and improve efficiency. If confirmed, I will work with the Department of Defense's leaders and medical professionals to address this challenge.

Promoting transparency of information that will help beneficiaries become more involved in making their healthcare decisions.

I strongly endorse this because it aids in the prevention of disease through an emphasis on healthy life-style decisions. Our service members and their families deserve the highest quality of medical care. If confirmed, I will ensure that the Military Heath System prioritizes transparency of information for service members and their families.

Mental Health Care

If confirmed, what actions would you take to ensure that sufficient mental health resources are available to service members in theater and to service members and families upon return to home station locations with insufficient community-based mental health resources?

We must consider both physical and mental health to be part of the resilience and effectiveness of the force. Furthermore, in light of the unique aspects of military service, we have a moral obligation to sustain the mental health of the force and of service members' families, just as we do their physical health. If confirmed, I will ensure that the Department of Defense is devoting appropriate resources to mental health, work with the Department of Veterans Affairs, and advise the Committee on what new approaches will be needed.

If confirmed, what would you do to ensure that robust mental health resources are available for Guard and Reserve members and their families?

Guard and Reserve members and their families have sacrificed a great deal over the last fifteen years of war. I will work to ensure that they have access to the mental health resources they need, and will advise the Committee if I learn that more resources are required.

Suicide Prevention

If confirmed, how would you maintain a strong focus on preventing suicides in the active and reserve components and in their families?

Every case of suicide is a tragedy. Moreover, suicide is a problem in our broader society, and is therefore reflected in our military, even though there are special stresses that apply to those in uniform. I have been educated on this issue by the work of Dr. Jonathan Shay. His research indicates that in the military unit cohesion, rigorous training, and humane leadership are factors that contribute to a reduction in rates of suicide. We have to build a military with humane personnel policies that enhance resilience and readiness. If confirmed, I will be unrelenting in addressing this issue with the Chairman and the Service Chiefs.

Personnel and Entitlement Costs

According to the Bipartisan Policy Center, military personnel costs, as a percentage of the overall DOD budget, have remained consistent for the last two decades at 30 percent while the size of the force continues to decrease. As a result, the one-third of the budget devoted to military personnel buys far less today than it did yesterday, despite the overall defense budget being significantly higher. In 1980, active-duty end strength was 2.1 million; this year, it is 1.3 million, a drop of over 60 percent.

If this percentage remains constant as overall defense spending flattens, or even declines in real terms, what would be the impact on the size of the force and the Department's ability to execute the national defense strategy?

We must support our force and structure our pay and benefits in a way that continues to benefit recruiting and retention—but the best support we can give service members is to equip and train them properly. Moreover, we owe it to the American people to field a force that can win. If the defense budget flattens or declines in real terms while this percentage remains constant, the Department of Defense will face major challenges in defending the nation's vital interests.

In your view, what would be the impact on other areas of the Department's budget if military personnel costs continue to rise while the overall defense budget remains flat, or even declines in real terms?

In 1980, pay for military personnel significantly lagged behind comparable jobs in the private sector. Since then, much progress has been made to increase military compensation to levels that can attract and retain a high quality all-volunteer force. If confirmed, I will examine this question in detail, but clearly personnel costs must be measured in conjunction with the other critical needs of the force.

What actions do you believe can and should be taken to control the rise in personnel costs and entitlement spending?

If confirmed, I will work with my team in the Office of the Secretary Defense, the Service Chiefs, and the Congress to identify options that can control costs while properly compensating the members of our fighting force.

Personnel Authorities

Do you believe that more flexibility is needed in the military personnel system? If so, what changes do you recommend to achieve personnel a system that is both flexible to the needs of service members and adaptable to future national security challenges?

Before changing any aspect of the Department's personnel policies, if confirmed I would need to review the specific military problem the change is meant to solve and then ask, "Will the change be consistent with maintaining the highest level of readiness for the force?" If confirmed, I will review the Force of the Future initiatives as a starting point to define any problems we face. After a more in-depth look at this issue, I will assess whether continued personnel reform is necessary and will work with the Congress on specific proposals.

Headquarters Reductions

The FY16 and FY17 NDAAs contain provisions aimed at reducing the bureaucracy in the Pentagon by reducing the number of management headquarters staff by 25% and by limiting the number of Senior Executive Service Officials and General and Flag Officers by about 12%.

Do you agree that bureaucracy in the Pentagon needs to be reduced?

I believe bureaucracy should be at the minimal level required to accomplish assigned tasks. At the same time, the role of the Department of Defense's civilian leadership is critical, and we must exercise a commitment to maintaining the principle of civilian control. The Pentagon's staff has evolved and grown over time because of efforts to limit contracted support, and to ensure that inherently governmental functions are performed by federal employees. I believe staff size should be based on assessments of the workforce needed to accomplish assigned tasks. I have a reputation for reducing bureaucracy: during my tenure at U.S. Joint Forces Command, I recommended and superintended its disestablishment.

Do you have any specific ideas for achieving the 25% reductions by means other than through a hiring freeze and attrition?

At this time, I do not have a refined understanding of all the tools currently at our disposal to shape and reshape the workforce. I am aware that the Department has a plan to comply with the statutory requirement, and if confirmed I would appreciate the Committee's support if we request additional tools to meet reduction targets though other more creative means.

Will you commit to working with this Committee and the Congress to pursue reforms to the civilian personnel system that emphasize growing the workforce needed to address the evolving challenges facing the Nation today and in the future?

Yes.

Religious Accommodation in the Military

In your view, do Department of Defense policies concerning religious

15

accommodation in the military appropriately accommodate the free exercise of religion and other beliefs, including individual expressions of belief, without impinging on those who have different beliefs, including no religious belief?

The free exercise of religion is one of the principles upon which our nation was founded, and it is my experience that the military places a high value on service members' rights to observe their beliefs. The religious practices of our service members should be accommodated consistent with our obligation to maintain operational readiness, standards, good order and discipline, and unit cohesion. If confirmed, I will ensure that this issue remains a priority for the Department of Defense.

Strategy

Please describe your views on how the United States currently develops and implements national security and defense strategies and how that process might be improved.

The National Defense Authorization Act for Fiscal Year 2017 establishes a requirement for a National Defense Strategy, developed with the advice of the Chairman of the Joint Chiefs of Staff and in support of the President's National Security Strategy. If confirmed, I will ensure that this process produces the meaningful, substantial results envisioned by the Congress.

The policy process must identify vital national security interests, and all military strategies developed to secure these interests should be regionally integrated and involve working with allies and with other elements of national power. Moreover, the Department of Defense should not emphasize one form of warfare at the exclusion of others, because the reality of war is that adversaries generally move against perceived weaknesses.

Detainee Treatment Policy

Do you support the standards for detainee treatment specified in the revised Army Field Manual on Interrogations, FM 2-22.3, issued in September 2006, and in DOD Directive 2310.01E, the Department of Defense Detainee Program, dated August 19, 2014, and required by Section 1045 of the National Defense Authorization Act for Fiscal Year 2016 (Public Law 114-92)?

I fully support using the Army Field Manual as the single standard for all U.S. military interrogations. I upheld that same standard before and after it was adopted in 2006.

Detention Facility at Guantanamo Naval Station

There are, as of December 9, 2016, 59 detainees remaining at the detention facility. Currently, the estimated cost of keeping an individual detainee at Guantanamo is approximately $7 million per year.

What are your views on the continued use of the detention facility at Guantanamo?

We have a legal right to capture enemy combatants and hold them as prisoners for the duration of a war. With regard to the detention facility at Guantanamo, I believe that we should develop a repeatable detainee policy that is appropriate for enemy combatants taken prisoner under such circumstances.

Do you believe the USG should be keeping detainees under long term detention, without prosecution or trial? Under what circumstances would long-term detention be appropriate?

Detention for the duration of hostilities to prevent a combatant's return to the battlefield is a fundamental precept of the law of armed conflict. Long-term detention is appropriate when an unprivileged enemy belligerent poses a continuing significant threat to the security of the United States.

Will you notify Congress if a decision is made to transfer a detainee to Guantanamo *before* the transfer occurs?

If confirmed, I will meet my obligations under applicable law to notify the Congress before the transfer or release of any detainees from Guantanamo Bay.

National Military Strategy and Stability Operations

The February 2015 National Security Strategy supports moving beyond the large ground wars in Iraq and Afghanistan and instead focuses on renewing our alliances from Europe to Asia.

In your opinion, while U.S. force presence has been reduced, to what extent are operations in Iraq and Afghanistan important to U.S. national security policy?

Problems arising in non-governed or terrorist-controlled areas are not confined there. 9/11 taught us a lesson we must not forget.

In your opinion, what are the primary lessons learned from the wars in Iraq and Afghanistan over the past decade?

First, we must remain engaged in the world. Second, unless we have a clear path to a better political end state, do not initiate regime change. Third, we must match military efforts with diplomatic and economic efforts. Fourth, we are strongest and our achievements most enduring when we work by, with, and through allies.

The January 2012 Defense Strategic Guidance called for U.S. forces to be ready to conduct limited counterinsurgency and other stability operations if required, and to retain and continue to refine the lessons learned, expertise, and specialized capabilities that have been gained over the past 10 years of operations in Iraq and Afghanistan. At the same time, the Strategic Guidance states that, "U.S. forces will no longer be sized to conduct large-scale, prolonged stability operations."

In your view, how should strategic guidance for the Department of Defense manage risk and articulate the types of missions or operations U.S. forces will or will not be expected to execute?

My view of the Department of Defense's strategic priorities is that we must first maintain a safe and secure nuclear deterrent. Second, we must field a decisive conventional force. Third, we must retain irregular warfare as a core competency of the U.S. military. This is an approach that prioritizes deterrence while giving us a shock absorber for the unexpected.

In your view, what are the appropriate roles and responsibilities, if any, of the Department of Defense in the planning and conduct of stability operations?

A critical role of the Department of Defense is to determine up front the likelihood of success in achieving the desired political end state following such an operation, and to determine the level of commitment in time and resources and the willingness required to sustain the effort and to achieve that end state.

What are the roles and responsibilities, if any, of the Department of Defense when coordinating with other departments and agencies of the Federal Government for the planning and conduct of stability operations?

It is my view that the Secretary of Defense must insist on a sufficient whole-of-government effort.

If confirmed, what adjustments, if any, would you recommend to the development of capabilities necessary for stability operations and to help prepare U.S. forces to conduct stability operations without detracting from their ability to perform combat missions?

If confirmed, I would work to strictly define the problems we are trying to solve, and advise the Committee and the President on my assessment of the Department of Defense's approach to stability operations. At this time, I believe that the military could benefit from improved education and training of the career force, with minor organizational changes for Foreign Internal Defense and mentoring units.

If confirmed, what recommendations would you make, if any, to improve the Department's approach to planning, resourcing, and conducting stability operations?

If confirmed, I look forward to examining this issue and working with the Committee on the Department of Defense's approach to stability operations.

Policy

What are the U.S. national security interests in Syria and what is your recommended strategy to address them?

If confirmed I will examine this complex issue in detail; it does not lend itself to a one or two paragraph answer. The brutal civil war in Syria has destabilized the Middle East, contributed to the destabilization of Europe, and threatened allies like Israel, Jordan, and Turkey, all while ISIS, Iran, and Russia have profited from the chaos—none of which has been in America's national interest. It is necessary to define the problems posed by the conflict, and to establish what level of priority we must assign to solving those problems in the midst of dealing with our other challenges.

What is your assessment of the national security challenges we face in Iraq?

Our principal interest in Iraq is to ensure that it does not become a rump state of the regime in Tehran and party to Iran's quest for regional hegemony—a quest that poses a threat to peace and stability. At the same time, we have a clear national interest in accelerating ISIS's defeat. Iran, however, has proven to be the primary source of turmoil in the Middle East, and any outcome should enable the Iraqi people to maintain their sovereignty vis-à-vis Iran.

What is the strategy needed to accomplish U.S. objectives in Iraq even after Mosul is liberated from ISIL?

It will be essential to fold any efforts in Iraq following ISIS's defeat in Mosul into an integrated regional strategy. If confirmed, I will prioritize the development of this strategy.

Senior U.S. Military officials have said Russia is the number one threat to the United States.

Please describe the challenges we face from Russia and the strategy required to address these concerns.

Russia has chosen to be a strategic competitor of the United States. That said, we engaged with Russia even during the darkest days of the Cold War, and I support the President-elect's desire to engage with Russia now. Engagement should serve as a means to achieve national objectives. We must define these objectives and look for areas of potential cooperation with Russia.

At the same time, when we identify other areas where we cannot cooperate, we must confront Russia's behavior, and defend ourselves if Russia chooses to act contrary to our interests. Challenges posed by Russia include alarming messages from Moscow regarding the use of nuclear weapons; treaty violations; the use of hybrid warfare tactics to destabilize other countries; and involvement in hacking and information warfare. Buttressing NATO will be fundamental to meeting these challenges, and we will need an integrated strategy that strengthens the North Atlantic Alliance and ensures that the Department of Defense is prepared to counter both traditional and emerging threats.

Do you support continued U.S. security assistance to Ukraine? If so, what strategy would you propose counter Russia's hybrid tactics which have employed both hard and soft power?

I support aid to Ukraine in support of their sovereignty. I owe a degree of confidentiality about my advice to the President-elect and would prefer to brief the Committee in Executive Session on this issue.

Iranian malign influence appears to continue to grow throughout the Middle East.

How do you assess the U.S. National security interests associated with the growth of Iranian influence in the Middle East?

Iranian malign influence in the region is growing. Iran is the biggest destabilizing force in the Middle East and its policies are contrary to our interests.

What policy objectives should we pursue in the Middle East and what strategy is necessary to achieve them?

Our strategy should be to support responsive governments throughout the region so that terrorism and extremism cannot grow and to checkmate Iran's goal for regional hegemony.

What are the U.S. National security interests and objectives in Afghanistan and what strategy do you recommend to achieve them?

We all remember what it felt like on 9/11 and 9/12. We should do what is necessary to prevent such an attack from occurring again.

Reconciliation

In your view, what should be the role of the United States in any reconciliation negotiations with the Afghan Taliban and other insurgent groups?

I understand that the State Department serves as the lead agency for coordinating U.S. reconciliation efforts in Afghanistan and that we support an Afghan-owned and Afghan-led reconciliation process with the Afghan Taliban and other insurgent groups. In the past, the Afghan Taliban were told that they must break ties with Al Qaeda, renounce violence, and abide by the Afghan Constitution in order to be allowed to enter the political process. I believe these continue to be reasonable demands, and that any U.S. role in such a process should be in support of U.S. national security interests, including the sovereignty of the government of Afghanistan.

What additional steps, if any, should the United States be taking to help advance the reconciliation process?

The U.S. is working with President Ghani and the government of Afghanistan to develop the capabilities of the Afghan National Defense and Security Forces. If confirmed, I will examine whether there are additional steps we should take to help advance the reconciliation process.

In your view, what should be the role of Afghanistan's neighbors, in particular Pakistan, in the reconciliation process? In your view, is Pakistan currently being helpful to the process?

I believe that states in the region have the responsibility to support the reconciliation process. From my time at U.S. Central Command, I am aware that the United States condemns any state support to the Taliban, whether it is moral or material in nature. States in the region should increase pressure on the Afghan Taliban and associated militant networks to stop their campaigns of violence in Afghanistan. Pakistan has learned some hard lessons because of its dealings with the Afghan Taliban, as violence in that country reflects, and I believe they should do more to collaborate with their neighbor. We should urge Pakistan to take further actions against the Taliban and the Haqqani Network.

Would you agree that the sanctuary for extremist forces in Pakistan is a key factor affecting the stability and security of Afghanistan? If so, what recommendations would you have to end this sanctuary?

Sanctuary and freedom of movement for the Afghan Taliban and associated militant networks inside Pakistani territory is a key operational issue faced by the Afghan security forces. If confirmed, I will examine efforts to deny sanctuary to the extremist forces undermining the stability and security of Afghanistan.

U.S. Strategic Relationship with Pakistan

What would you consider to be areas of shared strategic interest between the United States and Pakistan?

Areas of cooperation include our support for Pakistan's counter-terror and counter-insurgency efforts, Pakistan's approval of U.S. logistics movements into Afghanistan through its territory and airspace, and Pakistani support for counter-piracy activities in the Arabian Sea. I also understand that the United States has conducted military exercises with Pakistan in an effort to increase trust and interoperability.

If confirmed, what changes, if any, would you recommend for U.S. relations with Pakistan, particularly in terms of military-to-military relations?

Our relationship with Pakistan, including our military-to-military relationship, has had highs and lows. We have long faced a lack of trust within the Pakistani military and government about our goals in the region. If confirmed, I will work to build the trust that we need for an effective partnership.

U.S. Assistance to Pakistan

Since 2001, the United States has provided significant military assistance to Pakistan. In addition, the United States has provided significant funds to reimburse Pakistan for the costs associated with military operations conducted by Pakistan along the Afghanistan-Pakistan border, known as Coalition Support Funds.

Do you support conditioning U.S. assistance and other support to Pakistan on Pakistan's continued cooperation in areas of mutual security interest? If not, what changes would you recommend in security assistance to Pakistan?

For years, Pakistan has battled internally-focused extremist organizations within its borders and with our help. In a sign of its commitment, its military has suffered significant casualties in this counterinsurgency effort. Conditioning our security assistance has a mixed history in the case of Pakistan, but I will review all options if I am confirmed, and will consult with the Committee on this question. In particular, we should be aware of any behavior that supports Pakistan-based militant groups.

If such conditions prove to be ineffective in incentivizing Pakistan's cooperation in areas of mutual security interest, what options would you recommend for securing such cooperation?

If confirmed, I will work with the State Department and the Congress to incentivize Pakistan's cooperation on issues critical to our interests and the region's security, with a focus on Pakistan's need to expel or neutralize externally-focused militant groups that operate within its borders.

Africa

What is your assessment of the current counterterrorism strategy in Africa?

My perception is that the U.S. counterterrorism efforts in Africa have had some success in countering the threat posed by the leading terrorist organizations there, but that more could be done.

What changes, if any, would you recommend?

If confirmed, I would recommend that we have an integrated regional strategy that is tightly bonded with our allies, especially France, and that this strategy be linked with a global reassessment of our counterterrorism strategy.

U.S. Marine Corps Support to the State Department Embassy Evacuations

The Accountability Review Board for Benghazi supported the "State Department's initiative to request additional Marines and expand the Marine Security Guard (MSG) Program with corresponding requirements for staffing and funding. The Board also recommended that the State Department and DOD identify additional flexible MSG structures and request further resources for the Department and DOD to provide more capabilities and capacities at higher risk posts." The National Defense Authorization Act for Fiscal Year 2013 authorized up to 1,000 additional Marines in the MSG program to provide the additional end strength and resources necessary to support enhanced Marine Corps security at United States embassies, consulates, and other diplomatic facilities.

In your view, should the current arrangements between the Department of State and U.S. Marine Corps be modified?

At this time, I cannot see a reason to modify these arrangements.

In your view, would it be beneficial to the security of diplomatic facilities, many of which house U.S. military personnel, to have appropriate DOD personnel to assist in the conduct of vulnerability assessments of such facilities?

I have confidence in the professionalism and competence of Diplomatic Security personnel. If confirmed, I will provide full Department of Defense support to the Department of State to assist in vulnerability assessments of diplomatic facilities should such support be requested.

Collaboration between the Defense Department and the Intelligence Community

Since September 11, 2001, collaboration – both analytical and operational – between the Defense Department and the Intelligence Community has grown increasingly close. On one hand, seamless collaboration is a vital component of effective and rapid responses to non-traditional threats, and bringing together the strengths of the full spectrum of defense and intelligence missions creates opportunities for solutions

to complex problems. On the other hand, such collaboration – without effective management and oversight – risks blurring the missions of agencies and individuals that have cultivated distinct strengths or creating redundant lines of effort.

What are your views regarding the appropriate scope of collaboration between DOD and the Intelligence Community?

I believe in the tightest possible collaboration between the Department of Defense and the U.S. Intelligence Community. It is equally important for our intelligence agencies to maintain the independence of their assessments.

In your view, are there aspects of the current relationship between the Department and the Intelligence Community that should be re-examined or modified?

At this time, I'm not aware of any needed modification to the relationship. If confirmed I will be alert to the relationship and reexamine the need for change if necessary.

NATO Alliance

The reemergence of an aggressive Russia has resulted in the North Atlantic Treaty Organization (NATO) developing the Readiness Action Plan that NATO Secretary General Jens Stoltenberg called "the biggest reinforcement of our collective defense since the end of the Cold War." NATO also continues to be central to our coalition operations in Afghanistan and elsewhere.

In your view, particularly in light of the Russian Federation's aggression against Ukraine, what are the major strategic objectives of the NATO Alliance in the coming years?

NATO was constructed to reinforce Europe in the event of Soviet aggression. The first time the Alliance went to war was in defense of the United States after we were attacked on 9/11. I believe NATO is central to our defense. It facilitates European stability, and as a military alliance it helps sustain our values. Its objectives in coming years should include deterring aggression; projecting stability in accordance with the Alliance's interests; and promoting member contributions to the common defense, a long-standing issue of keen interest to multiple American institutions.

What are the greatest opportunities and challenges that you foresee for NATO in meeting its strategic objectives over the next five years?

The Alliance must harness renewed political will to confront and walk back aggressive Russian actions and other threats to the security of its members. It will face a critical challenge in maintaining solidarity on issues related to deterrence, defense, and the projection of stability in support of the North Atlantic community's interests.

In your opinion, does the NATO alliance benefit the national security interests of the United States?

Yes, enormously.

What steps, if any, would you recommend be taken to address potential shortfalls in Alliance capabilities?

In support of their national security, member states must share the burden of common defense, and meet or exceed the commitment to reach the two percent defense spending goal that their leaders set at the NATO summit in 2014. If confirmed, I will also encourage our NATO allies to spend their defense dollars more wisely—with appropriate and agreed shares devoted to procurement, research, and development—and to transform their forces for the threats we face today and in the future.

What do you see as the proper role, if any, for NATO in addressing the refugee and migrant threat in the Mediterranean Sea area?

In my view, the Alliance should support European governments and the European Union through information sharing and logistical support. I do not foresee a direct operational role for U.S. or NATO military forces at this time.

The concept of defense cooperation between NATO members was emphasized at the NATO summit in Chicago in May 2012.

What areas or projects would you recommend, if confirmed, that NATO nations cooperate in to improve NATO alliance capabilities?

In the near-term, NATO should emphasize increased readiness; missile defense; counter anti-access/area-denial capabilities; and combat enablers like command and control systems, precision munitions, and joint intelligence, surveillance, and reconnaissance capabilities.

Under what conditions, if any, would you envision further enlargement of NATO in the coming years?

Membership in NATO means the guarantee of Article 5 protection, so any additional defense burden on the Alliance should be carefully considered before an offer is made. New members must bring strength to the alliance, and their inclusion must result in a situation that is maintainable. With that said, all nations have the right to seek membership in any organization they choose. NATO has an open door if those nations meet these standards and the Alliance's other rigorous requirements for membership.

In your view, is there a continuing requirement for U.S. nuclear weapons to be deployed in NATO countries?

Yes. NATO has committed to remaining a nuclear Alliance for as long as nuclear weapons exist. Our NATO allies reaffirmed this stance at the Warsaw Summit last July, and I support the conviction that NATO must maintain an appropriate mix of nuclear, conventional, and missile defense capabilities.

If so, do you agree it is important to ensure that NATO's nuclear deterrence forces are survivable, well-exercised, and increasingly ready to counter Russian nuclear provocations?

Yes. The deterrence mission requires such readiness.

Do you support the continued deployment of the B61 weapon system for NATO and will you continue to support its modernization and continued deployment for use by NATO?

Yes. NATO's nuclear deterrence posture relies in part on U.S. nuclear weapons forward-deployed in Europe and on capabilities and infrastructure provided by NATO allies. As reaffirmed at Warsaw, the Alliance continues to endorse the current burden-sharing arrangements of which the B61 weapon system is an essential component.

If confirmed, will you continue to support making F-35 dual capable from a block four configuration for the U.S. and its allies in the shortest time possible?

The U.S. must continue to maintain the capability to forward-deploy strategic bombers and dual-capable aircraft as part of its nuclear and extended nuclear deterrence posture. If confirmed, I will take a careful look at this issue and consult with the Committee.

Please explain the consequences to our NATO allies if the block four configuration of the F-35 is not delivered in a timely fashion relative to their existing dual capable Tornados and F-16s.

As noted above, NATO's nuclear deterrence posture relies in part on U.S. nuclear weapons forward-deployed in Europe and on capabilities and infrastructure provided by NATO allies. These capabilities include dual-capable aircraft that contribute to current burden-sharing arrangements within NATO. In general, we must take care to maintain this particular capability, and to modernize it appropriately and in a timely fashion.

The fiscal year 2017 NDAA authorizes $3.4 billion for the European Deterrence Initiative (EDI) to support the stability and security of the region and deter further Russian antagonism and aggression.

In your opinion, what should the primary purposes of the EDI be and how successful has it been at accomplishing those purposes to date?

The primary purpose of the European Deterrence Initiative should continue to be improving the readiness and responsiveness of U.S. forces in the European theater, and building capacity in the Baltic States and Ukraine with the goal of deterring further aggressive Russian action. My understanding is that the Initiative has had a positive effect for NATO, as shown by the increased readiness of U.S. European Command forces compared to where they were three years ago.

What changes, if any, would you propose for future EDI efforts?

If confirmed, I will consult with the Chairman, the U.S. European Command Commander, and the Service Chiefs on what future efforts and investments will be appropriate, and advise the Committee on my conclusions.

Kosovo

Approximately 650 U.S. troops remain in the Balkans as part of the Kosovo Force (KFOR) that first deployed to Kosovo in 1999 and today is comprised of over 4,600 personnel from 30 countries.

What major lines of effort do you think are required to further reduce or eliminate U.S. and NATO presence in Kosovo?

Kosovo is an example of what happens when the international community, led by America, commits itself to the defense of its interests and values. In general, I would recommend reductions commensurate with the security situation on the ground, but my understanding is that, at present, the Force remains critical to ensuring the stability of the region. Moreover, before it would be prudent to reduce the U.S. military presence, the Kosovo Security Forces must receive a mandate to conduct domestic security and territorial defense, a shift that will require constitutional change with parliamentary support.

In your view, can the European Union play a more significant role in Kosovo?

Yes. The efforts of the European Union are essential to the economic and political development of Kosovo and its stability, and its further involvement ought to be encouraged. It already plays a significant role in Kosovo by brokering the normalization of relations between Serbia and Kosovo through the Belgrade-Pristina dialogue. The dialogue allows both countries to move forward with plans for membership in the European Union, with the understanding that recognition of Kosovo's sovereignty by Serbia will be addressed before actual membership accession. Additionally, the European Union helps contribute to stability in Kosovo through the European Rule of Law Mission in Kosovo.

Special Operations Forces

The FY 2017 National Defense Authorization Act included provisions designed to enhance the oversight and advocacy of special operations forces by the Assistant Secretary of Defense for Special Operations and Low Intensity Conflict (ASD SOLIC). Among other things, these reforms establish an administrative chain of command from the Commander of U.S. Special Operations Command through the ASD SOLIC to the Secretary of Defense, mirroring the relationship between the service secretaries and service chiefs.

What is your understanding of the "service secretary-like" responsibilities of the ASD SOLIC for special operations forces and, if confirmed, what would be your guidance to the ASD SOLIC for the fulfillment of these responsibilities?

I understand that the Department is working to better define these responsibilities, which would generally be similar to those of a secretary of a military department, including oversight over the readiness and organization of special operations forces, their resources and equipment, and associated civilian personnel. This provision deserves careful attention, and I look forward to working with Department personnel and the defense committees to understand its impact and how best to implement it.

In your view, how should these responsibilities be balanced with other responsibilities related to policy and operational issues?

The National Defense Authorization Act for Fiscal Year 2017 provides that the Assistant Secretary of Defense for Special Operations and Low Intensity Conflict reports directly to the Secretary, and has responsibility for special-operations administrative matters. The Assistant Secretary also reports to the Under Secretary of Defense for Policy for matters other than these special-operations-specific administrative matters. If confirmed, I will work with Department personnel and the defense committees to determine how best to implement this reporting structure.

Combating Terrorism

What is your assessment of the threat posed by ISIL, al Qaeda and other terrorist groups to the U.S. homeland, U.S. interests overseas, and Western interests more broadly?

Terrorist capabilities have been degraded, but they remain a threat to the U.S. homeland, our interests overseas, and Western interests more broadly. They intend to harm us and our allies. They will employ any means of violence at their disposal, including a weapon of mass destruction should they ever acquire one. We must retain the initiative and continue to degrade them to such a level as can be managed by law enforcement agencies.

What should be the guiding principles of the Department's efforts to combat these terrorist organizations and their adherents?

The Department of Defense should take action against terror groups who have the intent and capability to harm our homeland, citizens, or interests. Together with our allies and partners, we must grind such groups down to the point where law enforcement agencies can effectively handle them.

Do you support the killing or detention of the families of known terrorists even if they have no intelligence value or direct connection to terrorist activities?

No.

In your opinion, is the killing or detention of the families of known terrorists, even if they have no intelligence value or direct connection to terrorist activities, consistent with U.S. law and the Geneva Conventions?

No. The killing of non-combatants in a war against a non-state enemy violates Common Article 3 the Geneva Conventions. Legal questions aside, it is my view that such actions would be self-defeating and a betrayal of our ideals.

In your opinion, how important is the avoidance of civilian casualties to our overall strategy to combat terrorism and how must the risk of civilian casualties be weighed against taking direct action against terrorists?

Every decision to take direct action is unique and requires its own risk assessment. Unlike our enemies, we do everything humanly possible to prevent civilian deaths in war.

Section 1208 Operations

Section 1208 of the Ronald Reagan National Defense Authorization Act for Fiscal Year 2005 (Public Law 108-375), as amended by subsequent bills, authorizes the provision of support (including training, funding, and equipment) to regular forces, irregular forces, and individuals supporting or facilitating military operations by U.S. Special Operations Forces to combat terrorism.

What is your assessment of this authority?

It is my understanding that this provision affords the Secretary of Defense with a critical authority to support the fight against terror in a broad range of operational environments.

Defense Security Cooperation

What is the appropriate role of the Department of Defense in the conduct of security sector assistance?

Security cooperation extends beyond the military domain. However, the role of the Department of Defense in providing security assistance should be focused on ways to improve the military capacity of other states in order to help them become more reliable and effective partners with the U.S. on security matters. As we do so, we must be prepared to work with even imperfect allies and partner nations to defend our common interests.

What should be the strategic objectives of the Department of Defense's efforts to build the capabilities of a partner nation's security forces?

The Department's security assistance efforts should counter threats to American interests by enhancing the capacity of allies and partners to contribute to their own defense.

Is the Department of Defense appropriately organized and resourced to effectively conduct such activities? If not, what changes would you recommend?

If confirmed, I will look carefully at the Department's efforts to work by, with, and through allies and partners, and will advise the Committee if any changes are warranted.

Mass Atrocities Prevention

President Obama identified the prevention of mass atrocities and genocide as a core U.S. national security interest, as well as a core moral interest, in August 2011 under Presidential Study Directive 10.

What are your views on the role the United States plays in the prevention of mass atrocities and genocide?

It is my view that the United States can play an important role in the prevention of mass atrocities and genocide, depending on the circumstances. If confirmed, I will ensure that the Department of Defense adopts a whole-of-government approach while working with allies, partners, and international organizations on this issue. I will advise the Commander-in-Chief on what military action can realistically achieve in each situation.

What are your views on the adequacy of the Department's tools and doctrine for contributing to this role?

I believe that the tools and doctrine at our disposal are sufficient, should the Commander-in-Chief direct such an operation. If confirmed, should I find anything lacking in this regard, I will notify the Committee and provide recommendations.

U.S. Force Posture in the Asia Pacific Region

The Defense Department's January 2012 strategic guidance, "Sustaining U.S. Global Leadership: Priorities for the 21st Century", states that "while the U.S. military will continue to contribute to security globally, *we will of necessity rebalance toward the Asia-Pacific region.*" Likewise, the 2010 report of the Quadrennial Defense Review states that the United States needs to "sustain and strengthen our Asia-Pacific alliances and partnerships to advance mutual security interests and ensure sustainable peace and security in the region," and that, to accomplish this, DOD "will augment and adapt our forward presence" in the Asia-Pacific region.

What do you see as the U.S. security priorities in the Asia-Pacific region?

Our priorities in the Asia-Pacific region are consistent with our priorities in other regions: protecting our citizens and interests, strengthening our alliances and partnerships, and ensuring freedom of commerce and navigation on the global commons consistent with international law. As this is a primarily maritime theater, our naval forces, supported by other elements of the military, should be the centerpiece of the Department of Defense's integrated strategy for the region. Additionally, our alliances and partnerships in this region will be vital in preserving international law and deterring conflict.

Would you advise the new administration to continue the rebalance toward the Asia-Pacific region? If so, what does the term "rebalance" mean to you in terms of force structure, posture, basing, capabilities, and funding?

I hesitate to use phrases such as "rebalance" or "pivot" as they imply that we are turning away from our commitments elsewhere. We must be always prepared to defend this nation's interests wherever and whenever the President and the Congress direct. As I currently understand them, I believe our priorities in the region are sound, but if confirmed I will review them.

Overseas Basing Costs in Asia

Do you believe that the United States should withdraw forces from Japan and South Korea if those allies do not provide substantial additional support on top of the existing cost sharing arrangements in both countries? If so, where should these troops be based and at what additional expense?

I believe the United States is stronger when we uphold our treaty obligations, and when we stand by our allies and partners. We expect our allies and partners to uphold their obligations as well. If confirmed, I will consult with the Chairman of the Joint Chiefs and I will provide my best professional advice on any such proposals to the President. I look forward to working closely with this committee on all issues pertaining to overseas basing and the posture of our forces.

If there is a contingency in Japan or South Korea, how will the United States fulfill its treaty obligations to those nations without forward deployed troops in the region?

I know of no plan to withdraw forward deployed troops in the region. While such a move would present substantial challenges to our efforts to defend our interests and fulfill our obligations, the U.S. military is without peer in its ability to project power whenever and wherever necessary.

Ground Forces in the Pacific

Admiral Harris, the Commander of U.S. Pacific Command, and Deputy Secretary Work, have repeatedly articulated a need for the Army to develop myriad capabilities to "project power" beyond the ground domain into the air and maritime domains to anchor defenses in the Pacific and provide mutually supporting relationships among ground, naval, and air forces in the theater. The ability of ground forces to hold at risk adversary ships and aircraft; intercept missiles aimed at our ships, and at airfields, ports and other fixed facilities; and to provide electronic warfare and communications support for our air and naval forces could enable the United States to present adversaries with our own "anti-access/area denial" (A2AD) challenge.

Do you believe the current ground forces posture in Asia-Pacific is adequate? If not, what would you recommend to bolster it?

Given the maritime nature of the theater, the focus of our military strategy there should be the U.S. Pacific Fleet. The mission of our ground forces, whether that is the Army, the Marine Corps, or those of our partners and allies, is to support the fleet. If confirmed, I will work with the Chairman of the Joint Chiefs and our commanders in the region to determine if we need to adjust the posture of our ground forces so that they can accomplish any mission that they receive.

Do you concur that U.S. defense policy would be better served if the Army were to develop the capabilities and operational concepts for such a role, both for the European and the Pacific theaters?

If confirmed, I will examine this issue in detail, but as a general matter I believe that the Army should be resourced to operate as a decisive and lethal force in more than a single theater at a time.

Do you plan to continue the Guam Distributed Laydown Plan previously presented by the Department? If so, are you confident it can be executed at the current cost estimate and under the current political assumptions?

We should maintain a military posture in the region that is capable of persistent engagement with all countries in the Asia-Pacific. If confirmed, I will examine the progress of the laydown plan, which I understand is part of a long-standing agreement with Japan, and advise the Committee of my assessment.

What are the implications for the Third Offset given the recent push for a greater role for ground forces in the Pacific?

I understand the Department of Defense's Third Offset Strategy initiatives have focused on how to project combat power into any area at the time and place of our choosing. I also understand the Army and Marine Corps are working to ensure that ground forces can support any joint fight that might arise in the Pacific. If confirmed, I look forward to evaluating the state of the Third Offset Strategy initiatives, in combination with an evaluation of our current posture in the Asia-Pacific region and its alignment with our strategic interests.

Do you see a need for enhanced US security engagement in the Indian Ocean, and if so, in what areas and with whom?

Our global defense strategy must include robust capabilities to engage worldwide, and the Indian Ocean should be no exception. As one of the world's busiest trade corridors, the Indian Ocean is important to Asia's economic growth and global trade. We have a strong interest in ensuring safe and secure access to maritime routes there, and to a stable, peaceful, and prosperous region. India, Australia, Japan, and several of the Gulf Cooperation Council states are key partners for addressing the security challenges in this region, and it is my view that increasing our security assistance and military-to-military engagement with strategically positioned nations such as these is essential.

China

From your perspective, what effect is China's expanding economy and growing military having on the region at-large and how does that growth influence the U.S. security posture in the Asia-Pacific region?

As with my view of our approach to Russia, I believe we must seek to engage and collaborate with China where possible, but also be prepared to confront inappropriate behavior if China chooses to act contrary to our interests.

What can the U.S. do, both unilaterally and in coordination with allies and partners, to counter the increasing challenge posed by China in the East and South China Seas?

China's behavior has led countries in the region to look for stronger U.S. leadership. If confirmed, I will examine ways to strengthen our allies and partners, while taking a careful look at our own military capabilities in the region. We must continue to defend our interests there—interests that include upholding international legal rights to freedom of navigation and overflight.

Given that China's land reclamation in the South China Sea demonstrates a disregard for international rules and norms, do you support the UN Conventional on the Law of the Sea? Do you believe the United States should ratify the convention?

Upholding freedom of navigation and overflight world-wide are important U.S interests, and vital to the defense of our other national security interests. If confirmed, I will support policy measures designed to preserve and protect the continued global mobility of U.S. forces. I also note that the Law of the Sea Convention, to which many nations throughout the world are party, including China, largely reflects customary international law. If confirmed, I will keep these objectives and facts in mind in making any recommendations to the President and the Congress.

What are the national security implications for the United States of changing its one China policy?

The United States has long maintained its one-China policy, which is based on the three joint U.S.-China communiqués and the Taiwan Relations Act. This policy has been consistent across multiple administrations, both Republican and Democrat. If confirmed, I will provide to the President and the Congress my assessment of the current security situation in the Taiwan Strait and the likely consequences of any changes to U.S. policy.

North Korea

In your view, what should be the U.S. overall strategy to mitigate the threat posed by North Korea, to South Korea, to our allies in the region, and to the United States?

The United States must cooperate closely with our allies in the region, in particular the Republic of Korea and Japan, and work with other states with important interests in the situation, including Russia and China. We need to continue to strengthen our homeland and theater missile defense capabilities while working with our allies to strengthen their military capacity to deter and, if necessary, respond to aggression by North Korea. There should be no doubt of the U.S. resolve to defend our national security interests and those of our allies in the Asia-Pacific region. To address the longer-term issues associated with North Korea, I will work with the Secretary of State to craft the way ahead.

What is your assessment of the current security situation on the Korean peninsula?

The security situation on the Korean peninsula remains volatile as a result of continued provocative statements and actions by the North Korean leadership. These include the expansion of its nuclear weapons program, continued development of increasingly sophisticated ballistic missile capabilities, and repeated threats to the

34

U.S. and its allies in the region.

If confirmed, will you report back to this committee on actions you will take to ensure United States Forces Korea has the capability to defeat sites in North Korea containing weapons of mass destruction? In doing so, will you report actions from both a conventional forces perspective and from one working with the interagency, such as the Department of Energy, for those sites in particular that process, handle, or store special nuclear material?"

Yes.

India

Congress strongly supports an enhanced defense relationship between the United States and India.

What is your view of the current state of the U.S.-India security relationship?

India is the world's largest democracy, and our relationship with it is of the utmost importance. In my view, and particularly on security and defense issues, the U.S.-India relationship has been strengthened in recent years. Cooperation on defense trade and technology has grown to the benefit of both countries under the Defense Technology and Trade Initiative. I also believe that India's "Act East" policy allows it to play a greater role in contributing to security in the Asia-Pacific region.

What would be your strategy for bolstering the overall defense relationship between our two countries? Which areas would you focus on? If confirmed, what specific priorities would you establish for this relationship?

U.S. policy should continue to pursue a long-term strategic relationship with India based on the convergence of our interests and our shared democratic values. I note that the United States and India recently cemented India's status as a Major Defense Partner. If confirmed, I would assess what particular areas in the bilateral security relationship I should focus on, and what steps can be taken to bolster the overall defense relationship.

Department of Defense Counternarcotics Activities

DOD serves as the single lead agency for the detection and monitoring of aerial and maritime foreign shipments of drugs flowing toward the U.S. On an annual basis, DOD's counternarcotics (CN) program expends nearly $1 billion to support the Department's CN operations, including building the capacity of U.S. Federal, State, and local law enforcement agencies, and certain foreign governments, and providing intelligence support on CN-related matters and a variety of other unique enabling capabilities.

In your view, what is the appropriate role of DOD in counterdrug efforts?

Drug trafficking and transnational organized crime threaten U.S. national security interests, and the public health crisis associated with the abuse of illicit narcotics is of national concern. Combating these threats requires all elements of the government to work together, and I am aware of the important role played by the Department of Defense. If confirmed, I will review the Department's contributions to these efforts and advise the President and the Committee as appropriate.

Do you believe that the U.S. broadly, and the U.S. military more narrowly, have been effective in achieving counterdrug objectives?

The Department's counternarcotics efforts have disrupted the flow of illegal drugs, and they have strengthened partner nations' abilities to counter instability generated by the drug trade. Colombia's success in combatting drug-fueled terrorism is one example. As noted above, if confirmed, I will review the Department's contributions and advise the President and the Committee as appropriate.

In your view, what should be the role of the United States in countering the flow of narcotics to nations other than the U.S.?

As a former Commander of U.S. Central Command and a field commander in Iraq and Afghanistan, I have seen how drug trafficking serves as an important revenue source for terrorist organizations and other threat networks. We should continue to support international efforts to disrupt drug trafficking. This is especially important in Afghanistan, where the Taliban derives significant revenue from producing and trafficking heroin to markets such as Europe and Central Asia.

Western Hemisphere

What should be the Department's strategic priorities in the Western Hemisphere?

The Department's strategic priorities in the Western Hemisphere should be, first and foremost, to defend the homeland, our allies, and our national interests. The Department should continue to work closely with Canada, including through the North American Aerospace Defense Command, and with other partners in Latin America and the Caribbean to expand our partners' roles as contributors to international security, assisting them in professionalizing their security forces and institutions. The Department should also support Colombia's implementation of a successful peace accord; support broader U.S. interagency efforts to counter violence and corruption, particularly in Central America; and advance hemispheric and regional cooperation on shared security challenges.

Is the Department appropriately resourced to support these priorities? If not,

where do you assess the Department is accepting the greatest risk?

If confirmed, I will assess our priorities and determine which areas, if any, require new guidance, additional resources, or further measures to mitigate risk.

Cuba

On December 17, 2014, President Obama announced changes in the diplomatic relationship between the U.S. and Cuba, which includes the easing of several longstanding restrictions.

Would you recommend the establishment of military-to-military engagement between the U.S. and Cuba? If so, what, if any, prerequisites should there be to their establishment?

No.

What are the areas in which U.S. and Cuban security interests overlap? Do you think it would be beneficial to U.S. security interests to seek to cooperate on areas of overlap?

Significant differences between the U.S. and Cuba would have to be addressed before I could recommend that the Department of Defense explore security cooperation with its Cuban counterparts.

Strategic Reviews

What is your understanding and assessment of the Department's processes for analysis, developing each of the following strategic reviews:

The Defense Strategy Review (section 118 of title 10, United States Code, as amended by Public Law 113-291););

The National Military Strategy (section 153 of title 10, United States Code); and

Global Defense Posture Review (section 2687a of title 10, United States Code)

My current understanding is that these strategic reviews add value. If confirmed, I will be able to provide the Committee with more specific feedback on the process of developing strategy, including the role of specific strategic reviews. In general, I believe properly developed strategies are critical to guide effective action.

If confirmed, what recommendations would you make, if any, to change title 10, United States Code, and to improve DOD's processes for analysis, policy formulation, and decision making relative to each review above?

While there is value to the current scheme of strategy and posture reviews, my sense is that the Secretary of Defense ought to have a single document to evaluate the strategy and posture of the Department. Moreover, both the review process and the vital communication of the process's results to the Congress could, in general, benefit from streamlining and consolidation. If confirmed, I look forward to providing the committee with my detailed assessment of this issue.

Munitions

To comply with current DoD Policy on Cluster Munitions and Unintended Harm to Civilians, after December 31, 2018 the United States military will no longer employ cluster munitions containing submunitions that result in more than 1% unexploded ordnance.

What is your view on the current cluster munitions policy?

Cluster munitions continue to be an integral part of U.S. force capabilities. When used appropriately, in accordance with the law of armed conflict, those cluster munitions with a low unexploded ordnance rate afford critical advantages against certain categories of legitimate military targets. Used properly, these weapons can generate less collateral damage than high explosive unitary weapons. My view is that U.S. policy on cluster munitions should continue to strike a balance between maintaining lawful and legitimate military capabilities and reducing the potential of unintended harm to non-combatants.

What is your assessment of the ability of the United States military to meet its combat requirements after December 31, 2018 under the conditions of the current policy, particularly on the Korean peninsula?

I am not presently in a position to give an appropriately detailed answer to this question. If confirmed, identifying and mitigating any vulnerabilities to our defense posture caused by the current cluster munitions policy will be a priority.

Defense Capabilities

The original discretionary caps imposed by the Budget Control Act (BCA) will be in effect for FY 2018 through FY 2021, unless there is agreement to change budget levels.

In your assessment, what would be the impacts of continued implementation of the BCA discretionary caps through 2021 on the Department of Defense and national security? And in particular how would end strength, capacity, capabilities, and readiness be effected?

As I noted earlier, I believe the continued implementation of such caps would require a recalibration of our ability to assert U.S. influence across the world. We are already seeing the adverse impact of dramatically reduced budgets. Readiness and modernization have also been casualties of reduced funding in a threat environment that demands continued engagement.

What do you believe are the appropriate end strength levels for the Army, Navy, and Air Force to reach by 2022?

The President-elect has spoken about the end strength levels of the services, and, if confirmed, I will give him my best advice on this issue. I will also work with the Chairman and the Service Chiefs to develop recommendations on current and future end strength plans for their services consistent with the President-elect's national security strategy.

How would you propose achieving those levels with a focus on continuing to recruiting high quality candidates?

The rate of any end strength increases must be carefully balanced against the importance of recruiting and retaining high quality candidates.

What is your opinion on the necessity to modernize our weapons systems in light of current and emerging threats?

The technology of warfare is constantly evolving as competitors seek to gain or sustain competitive advantages. For the U.S., we must have the capability to deter conflict and, should deterrence fail, to win. If confirmed by the Senate, one of my chief responsibilities as Secretary will be to ensure our weapon systems remain the best against those fielded by any competitor so that our troops never go into a fair fight. This will involve establishing a culture of innovation across the Department, and encouraging the adoption of proven capabilities, rather than seeking to reinvent what already exists on the commercial market.

What are the most critical capabilities the Department needs to prioritize over the next 10 years?

We must maintain a robust nuclear deterrent and lethal conventional forces, while ensuring that irregular warfare remains a core capability. The Department must also enhance its cyber and space-based capabilities to ensure we project strength in all domains of warfare.

How will you keep defense acquisition costs under control and ensure the American taxpayer receives the absolutely best defense capabilities for their precious and scarce defense dollars?

It is imperative to assess the cost, schedule, and performance of programs to ensure they are meeting warfighting needs at an affordable cost. The acquisition system and culture must adapt to the reality that hardware and software systems must be integrated and change on a more frequent basis in order to meet warfighter needs, adapting to the speed of relevance. The Department should not waste time and money trying to duplicate capabilities that already exist on the commercial market. If confirmed, I will select acquisition professionals capable of implementing best practices while embracing competition as an essential component of product procurement and development.

Navy Shipbuilding

President-elect Trump has vowed to rebuild the U.S. Navy toward a goal of 350 ships. The Navy's current naval battle force is only 273 ships, and will not reach the previous Navy goal of 308 ships until 2021 and there is no current plan for reaching the Navy's new goal of 355 ships.

In a November 2016 report, the Congressional Research Service (CRS) found achieving and maintaining a notional 349 ship force structure would require adding on the order of 45 to 58 ships to the Navy's FY2017 30-year shipbuilding plan, or an average of about 1.5 to 1.9 additional ships per year, at a cost of roughly $3.5 billion to $4.0 billion per year over the 30-year period.

> **In your view, how large a Navy, consisting of what mix of ships, will be needed in coming years to adequately perform Navy missions?**

> **What steps are you considering recommending the President-elect take to realize his goal of a 350 ship Navy, particularly related to additional ship procurement and the funding required?**

> **What is your understanding of the similarities and differences between the new Administration's 350 ship goal and the Navy's new 355 ship requirement?**

> The President-elect has established goals for our Navy's force structure, and I support the increases in Naval combatants compared to current plans. Our shipbuilding plan must be driven by the requirements of our national security strategy. I note that the President-elect's call for a 350 ship Navy is very close to the results of the Navy's recent Force Structure Assessment. If confirmed I will work with the Congress on all aspects of this issue, including procurement, timing, funding, cost-control, and our strategic requirements for specific ship numbers and classes of ships.

The Navy has begun acquiring the replacements for the Ohio class ballistic missile submarines (SSBNs). The new Ohio class replacement boats are projected to have an acquisition cost of $10 billion per ship. The Navy has stated publicly that it could not afford to buy both the new SSBNs and maintain other required procurements under Defense Department budget top lines that would be consistent with the defense discretionary spending caps within the Budget Control Act.

What priority will you place on the Ohio class Replacement Program in relation

to other acquisition programs?

Do you believe the Navy can expand to a 350-ship fleet, while also procuring the Ohio class replacement SSBNs?

The Ohio class replacement program is an essential element of a credible and safe nuclear deterrent. The ballistic missile submarine capability is the most survivable leg of the nuclear triad and deserves prioritization accordingly. The reductions and restrictions imposed by the sequester levels are severe and have forced choices that have reduced our conventional naval capabilities while still not permitting modernization of our nuclear deterrent. We must remove the sequester and, if confirmed, I will work closely with the Committee—which continues to be a leader on this issue—in concert with the President-elect.

In the 1970s and 1980s, the Nation procured the current Ohio class SSBN submarines within the Navy's shipbuilding (SCN) account. In 2015, Congress created a special fund, the National Sea-Based Deterrence Fund (NSBDF), for procurement of Ohio class replacement SSBNs.

Recognizing these submarines perform a national mission, how do you believe the cost of Ohio class replacement SSBNs should be funded – solely from Navy resources, from a combination of Navy and other-than-Navy (e.g., OMB and other Defense) sources, or with a different approach? Please explain.

If confirmed, I will work with the Defense Comptroller, the Office of Management and Budget, and the Congress to determine the best way to manage and exercise responsible stewardship of funds allocated for this program.

Aircraft Carriers

After more than $2 billion in cost growth in each of the first three Ford-class aircraft carriers, the costs of these ships range from $11.4 billion to $12.9 billion.

In your view, should the Navy pursue smaller, less expensive aircraft carriers to complement the Ford and Nimitz class aircraft carriers?

The Navy's large deck carrier program has been a critical element of our country's ability to project power. If confirmed, I will work with the Chairman and the Chief of Naval Operations to provide recommendations to the President-elect and the Committee regarding the future force structure of the Navy.

The delivery date of CVN-78 was last announced to be November 2016 and the Navy is currently not providing a delivery date, due primarily to complications with the propulsion plant and testing of that system.

What is your understanding of the reasons behind the CVN-78 delivery delay,

potential for further cost growth, and the timeline for delivering this ship?

In my capacity as a private citizen, I have not had access to recent, detailed information on this issue. If confirmed, I will carefully study the data on this program and provide details to the Committee.

Littoral Combat Ship (LCS)

In February 2016, the Secretary of Defense announced his decision to down-select to a single LCS variant and reduce the procurement quantity to 40 LCS or LCS frigates, as codified in revision 3 of the LCS acquisition strategy signed in March 2016. Section 123 of the Fiscal Year 2017 National Defense Authorization Act prohibits revisions or deviations from this acquisition strategy unless the Secretary of Defense submits a certification to the congressional defense committees.

Do you support Secretary Carter's decision to modify the LCS program, specifically to require a down-select to a single LCS variant and reduce the total procurement quantity to 40 ships? If not, please explain your views.

I have not had access to the detailed assessments available to Secretary Carter before he made this decision. If confirmed, I will review the Navy's Littoral Combat Ship program and the issue of the down-select, and advise this Committee on my findings.

The initial operational capabilities for the 3 LCS mission modules, which give the ships combat capabilities, are delayed by a cumulative of 26 years – 5 years for the surface warfare package (occurred 2015), 9 years for the anti-submarine warfare module (expected 2019), and 12 years for the mine countermeasures package (expected 2020) – creating a significant mismatch between the 26 LCS on contract and their ability to deploy combat capabilities.

Do you consider the current situation of 26 LCS on contract with practically no proven combat capability acceptable?

I will need to conduct a detailed review of this program if confirmed.

Would you consider halting procurement of further LCS seaframes at least until all 3 modules have achieved an initial operational capability?

As noted above, I have not been privy to the sort of details and internal assessments that would have to inform such a decision, and I owe it to the President-elect and the Committee to investigate what is clearly a serious problem before offering specific solutions.

Army Modernization

What is your understanding and assessment of the Army's record with respect to

equipment modernization?

What are the challenges facing the Army in its effort to modernize weapons systems?

What actions, if any, would you take to ensure that the Army achieves a genuinely stable, achievable, and affordable modernization strategy and program?

What is your understanding and assessment, if any, of the Army's recently established Strategic Portfolio Analysis Review (SPAR) effort that is focused on reviewing capabilities within portfolios and prioritizing its long-term investment strategies?

What actions, if any, would you take to sustain the momentum of these reviews in stabilizing the Army's modernization strategy and priorities?

It is my understanding that the Army modernization posture is complicated by the sequester, which has forced Army leaders to scale back their plans in this area. Our Army must be equipped, trained, and ready for combat, now and in the future. Like the other services, the Army must continually assess the relevance of its capabilities against current and projected threats, adjust to the resources available to it, and then determine whether to update current platforms to both improve and extend their capability, pursue wholly new capabilities, or both. Since major platforms are kept in the inventory for decades, it is important to ensure they meet operational needs for a substantial period of time. If confirmed, I will have access to the details of the Army's on-going reviews and their assessments of needed capabilities, and would then be able to provide more informed comment on the details of this issue.

Small Arms and Ammunition

The most deployed weapon system of the last fifteen years of war is the assigned individual weapons of Soldiers and Marines. Despite years of wartime budget increases and lessons learned from thousands of ground combat engagements with the enemy, the small arms and ammunition used by the Army and Marine Corps today are roughly the same as they were in 2001 with few exceptions. Unclassified reports show small arms capabilities of threat nations that outmatch what the average American infantry soldier or marine takes to battle today.

If confirmed, how will you rapidly modernize and improve the Army and Marine Corps small arms weapons and ammunition?

I am aware that both the Army and Marine Corps have conducted a series of reviews of their basic service weapons and are both involved in ongoing reviews of their service rifle, in particular, and related ammunition. If confirmed, I will ensure the Service Chiefs receive the support they need to fulfill their Title 10 responsibilities to equip their troops for success on the battlefield. I look forward to discussing these matters with the Committee at the appropriate time.

Unfunded Priorities

Section 1003 of the FY13 NDAA expressed the sense of Congress with respect to the annual submission by the Service Chiefs and Commander of U.S. Special Operations Command of their critical unfunded priorities that are not included in the President's annual budget request.

If confirmed, will you allow the Service Chiefs and Commander, U.S. Special Operations Command to comply with this sense of Congress?

Yes.

Space

What do you perceive as the threats to our national security space satellites?

The threat to our satellite capabilities is real and growing. Both China and Russia have developed and tested a variety of anti-satellite weapons that can destroy or disable satellites.

Briefly describe what policy objectives we should be seeking to achieve and the strategy you think is necessary to address these threats.

We must ensure the availability, security, and resiliency of our assets at all times and through all phases of conflict.

Do you support the development of offensive space control capabilities to counter those threats?

Offensive space control capabilities should be considered to ensure survivable and resilient space operations necessary for the execution of war plans. If confirmed, I will examine the feasibility of integrating such considerations into existing national security policy.

The Fiscal Year 2017 National Defense Authorization Act prohibits the use of Russian rocket engines after December 31, 2022. Are you committed to ending our dependence on the use of Russian rocket engines as soon as possible, perhaps even before December 31, 2022?

If confirmed, I will comply with the law, and work in consultation with the Congress to meet or exceed any deadline requirements it imposes.

Cyber

How do you perceive the challenges we face in cyberspace?

The challenges we face are significant and varied, and activities by our adversaries are increasing in complexity, severity, and frequency. The Department of Defense must be part of a whole-of-government effort to ensure our nation's interests are preserved in the cyber domain.

Briefly describe what policy objectives we should be seeking to achieve and the strategy you think is necessary to address these challenges.

We need to develop a clear whole-of-government policy regarding our response to cyber aggression, while hardening our information networks and critical infrastructure. The Department of Defense must continue to develop the military forces and capabilities needed to deter our adversaries and protect the nation's security in the cyber domain, while providing options for the President. Specifically, we must improve our offensive and defensive capabilities, and our ability to identify accurately the sources of attacks. We must also ensure we are recruiting and retaining the sort of personnel we need to meet the highly technical challenges posed by this domain of warfare.

What are your views about elevating U.S. Cyber Command to a unified command and about maintaining or ending the "dual hat" relationship where the Commander of Cyber Command serves also as the director of the National Security Agency?

At this time, I support elevating Cyber Command to a unified command. I understand that, if confirmed, my certification and that of the Chairman of the Joint Chiefs is required before the current dual-hat arrangement can be changed. I will give this issue careful personal attention.

Do you believe we are deterring our adversaries in cyberspace? If not, what do you believe will be necessary to deter our adversaries in cyberspace?

No. To be deterred, our adversaries must know they will suffer consequences from cyber attacks that outweigh any gains they hope to achieve. If they choose to act as adversaries, we will treat them as such.

What do you believe would constitute an act of war in cyberspace?

My understanding is that currently such a determination is to be made on a case-by-case basis by the President. I further note that a cyber attack does not need to be deemed an "act of war" to warrant a response. As the Committee has recently heard in expert testimony, we still lack a comprehensive cyber doctrine. If confirmed, I am committed to working with other elements of the government to develop a reinvigorated national strategy for responding to challenges in the cyber domain.

China's Aggressive Theft of U.S. Intellectual Property

A recent report by the National Counterintelligence Executive confirmed that China is engaged in a massive campaign to steal technology, other forms of intellectual property, and business and trade information from the United States through cyberspace. The previous Commander of U.S. Cyber Command has referred to this as the greatest transfer of wealth in history and, along with others, believes this is a serious national security issue.

Do you believe that China's aggressive and massive theft of technology in cyberspace is a threat to national security and economic prosperity?

Yes. China's misappropriation of American secrets and intellectual property poses a significant risk to our national security.

The FY 2015 NDAA authorized the President to impose sanctions, pursuant to the International Emergency Economic Powers Act (50 U.S.C. 1701 et seq.), on persons determined to knowingly request, engage in, support, facilitate, or benefit from economic or industrial espionage in cyberspace against United States persons.

What are your views on the potential impact of this legislation?

I am not an expert in the delegation of this specific authority, but the issue it is designed to address is important.

What additional steps do you believe are needed to deter China from such activities in the future?

Any such steps must be part of an integrated regional strategy for the Asia-Pacific, and take into account a national strategy for responding to challenges in the cyber domain. If confirmed, I will advise the Committee as the Department of Defense refines its approach on this issue.

DOD's Role in Defending the Nation from Cyber Attack

What is your understanding of the role of the Department of Defense in defending the Nation from an attack in cyberspace? In what ways is this role distinct from those of the homeland security and law enforcement communities?

Consistent with its core responsibility to defend the nation, the Department of Defense is responsible for defending the United States against attacks and other malicious activities in the cyber domain. The Department is also responsible for defending its own networks against such activities, including cyber attacks and espionage.

The Department also works closely with the Department of Homeland Security and the Department of Justice as they carry out their own responsibilities. Homeland Security is the lead Department for protecting, mitigating, and recovering from domestic cyber incidents in accordance with established policy. The Department of Justice investigates, attributes, disrupts, and prosecutes cybercrimes that fall outside of military jurisdiction, and it provides domestic response to national security incidents. When directed, the Department of Defense, including through the National Guard, can provide support to State and local governments and to the private sector.

Next Challenges in Growing Operational Cyber Capabilities

The Department of Defense, in a significant milestone in the maturation of the cyber warfare mission, is successfully organizing and training personnel for units to conduct military operations in cyberspace.

What challenges does the Department face in developing the command and control, operational planning, mapping and situational awareness, battle damage assessment, tools and weapons, and infrastructure capabilities necessary to conduct large-scale operations in cyberspace?

It is my understanding that the Cyber Mission Force is the principal entity for the defense of Department of Defense information networks, the defense of the Nation from cyber attacks and malicious activities, and the provision of cyberspace options for the Combatant Commands. If confirmed, I will carefully examine its work and advise the President and the Congress on what progress the Department is making.

Nuclear Weapons and Stockpile Stewardship

What is the role of U.S. nuclear weapons?

To deter nuclear war and to serve as last resort weapons of self-defense. In this sense, U.S. nuclear weapons are fundamental to our nation's security and have historically provided a deterrent against aggression and security assurance to U.S. allies. A robust, flexible, and survivable U.S. nuclear arsenal underpins the U.S. ability to deploy conventional forces worldwide; provides the Commander-in-Chief with credible response options to strengthen deterrence; and supports U.S. nonproliferation goals by extending deterrence to allies, thereby dissuading them from developing their own nuclear weapons.

The President's June 2013 Nuclear Employment Strategy affirmed that the United States will maintain a nuclear triad, noting that "Retaining all three TRIAD legs will best maintain strategic stability at reasonable cost, while hedging against potential technical problems or vulnerabilities."

Do you agree that modernizing each leg of the nuclear triad and the DoE nuclear weapons complex is a critical national security priority?

As our civilian and uniformed leaders have testified consistently and over the course of many administrations, ensuring the continued effectiveness of deterrence through the maintenance of a robust, reliable, flexible, and survivable nuclear arsenal is a paramount national security priority. We must continue with current nuclear modernization plans for all three legs of the Triad, and for associated command and control systems.

Will you continue to support the Long Range Standoff Weapon (LRSO) and its timely replacement of the AGM-86 Air-Launched Cruise Missile?

I will carefully examine the utility and advisability of this program within existing nuclear doctrine and report back to the Committee with an informed answer.

Cooperative Threat Reduction Program

What are your views of the Cooperative Threat Reduction Program?

The Nunn-Lugar Cooperative Threat Program has been successful in dismantling and eliminating a range of weapons-of-mass-destruction threats from the former Soviet Union. Although the Russian Federation did not renew the umbrella agreement that would have allowed this program to continue within Russia, the program accomplished many of its primary objectives.

If confirmed, will you ensure it is capable of meeting its mission to roll back the threat of weapons of mass destruction?

If confirmed, I will work to maximize the effectiveness of the Department's Cooperative Threat Reduction activities, and I will work to enhance cooperative measures with other states to reduce the weapons-of-mass-destruction threat.

Russian Violation of the 1987 INF Treaty

In your view, what are the consequences for U.S. national security of Russia's actions in violation of its obligations under the INF Treaty?

The violation of the INF Treaty by the Russian Federation increases the risk to our allies and poses a threat to U.S. forces and interests. If Russia is permitted to violate the treaty with impunity, such actions could erode the foundations of all current and future arms control agreements and initiatives.

What do you believe would be appropriate responses for the United States to take in order to: (a) convince Russia to return to compliance with the INF Treaty, or (b) ensure that U.S. national security is maintained if Russia does not return to compliance?

Russia's violation of the treaty will lead to no significant military advantage. Returning to compliance is in Russia's best interest. When Russia chooses to act as an adversary, we must respond appropriately and in league with our allies.

Ballistic Missile Defense

The United States homeland and its deployed forces enjoy a measure of protection against ballistic missile threats from rogue nations such as North Korea and Iran, yet the threat continues to grow. During the past year, North Korea conducted several missile tests and continued development of mobile long-range missiles. Likewise, Iran continues to test ballistic missiles of increasing range. Russia and China also continue to deploy ballistic, cruise, and hypersonic missiles that threaten U.S. forces, allies and the U.S. homeland.

What are your priorities for U.S. missile defense capabilities in the following areas: a) homeland missile defense; b) regional missile defense; c) improved discrimination and sensors; d) next generation missile defense; and e) defense against cruise and hypersonic missiles?

Homeland defense and protecting our forces abroad should be the first priority for our missile defense capabilities. The next priority should be to work with our allies to aid them where necessary, and to help them build their own defenses. If confirmed, I will identify those areas where additional investments may be needed, and determine which investments can produce the best returns in a timely manner.

Do you believe that the U.S. should encourage our regional allies and partners to increase their missile defense capabilities to contribute to regional security and help reduce the burden on U.S. forces and requirements?

Yes. The proliferation of ballistic missiles that can carry weapons of mass destruction is a growing threat to U.S. allies and partners. Efforts of our regional allies and partners in this area are welcome, and if I am confirmed I will encouraged such efforts.

Medical Countermeasures Initiative (MCMI)

The Administration has produced an interagency strategy for the advanced development and manufacture of medical countermeasures (MCM) to defend against pandemic influenza and biological warfare threats. In this strategy, the Department of Defense will be responsible for the rapid development and manufacture of medical countermeasures to protect U.S. Armed Forces and Defense Department personnel.

Do you support this interagency strategy and the MCM Initiative and, if confirmed, would you plan to implement them?

I am not currently familiar with this strategy, but the issue it addresses is critical. If confirmed, I will review this issue and provide my assessment to the Committee.

Efficiency in Department Operations

In your view, what latitude must be given to the Joint Chiefs to enact cost-saving reforms?

The Joint Chiefs, as well as all Department of Defense personnel, should be encouraged to identify and implement cost saving reforms. We must also implement policies to reward cost-saving elements. If confirmed, I intend to meet with the Service Chiefs, as well as the civilian leaders in the Office of the Secretary of Defense and the military departments, to solicit their advice on achieving cost savings, and to encourage them to eliminate redundancies and give strong attention to the Defense Business Board study of January 2015.

Base Realignment and Closure (BRAC)

Do you believe that a BRAC round is needed and, if so, what changes to the law would you request to ensure that we don't have a repeat of the 2005 BRAC?

I have not been privy to BRAC discussions at the level of the Secretary's office and the Congress, although I will note that the Congress's intent in the National Defense Authorization Act of 2017 is clear.

Global Basing

On January 27, 2015, you testified before the Committee that "Today we have less of a military shock absorber to take surprise in stride, and fewer forward-deployed military forces overseas to act as sentinels."

In your opinion, how important is access to basing locations in foreign countries and forward deployed forces to addressing the threat from near-peer competitors, terrorist groups, and other contingencies that may arise?

Access to bases is one of the principal benefits of security alliances and partnerships, enabling us to act in concert with allies and partners. Forward-deployed military forces have historically either deterred emerging situations or resolved them before they developed into full-blown crises. When crises do require follow-on forces, access and basing agreements are vital capabilities for any military campaign.

In your opinion, how important are the relationships with foreign partners and host countries to maintaining such a forward presence?

Established relationships with allies and partners are indispensable in preserving an effective forward presence. These relationships must be built upon a foundation of common cause, earned trust, mutual respect, and personal familiarity. Consequently, whenever possible such relationships of trust must be established in advance of a crisis.

Unified Command Plan

What is your understanding and assessment of the current Unified Command Plan? In your view, is there a need to undertake a major reevaluation toward modification of the current Unified Command Plan? If so, explain why.

I need to review the current document and, if confirmed, I will advise the Committee if I believe changes are warranted.

In your view, are there opportunities for greater effectiveness and efficiencies by the consolidation of the roles and responsibilities two or more current geographic combatant commands, such as U.S. Northern Command and U.S. Southern Command? If not, please explain why.

I am willing to consider reevaluations of our current command and headquarters structure. Any such proposals must clearly identify the problem they are intended to solve.

Test and Evaluation (T&E)

If confirmed, will you make it a priority to ensure that the Department as a whole and each of the Services specifically maintains its testing organizations, infrastructure, and budgets at levels adequate to address both our current and future acquisition needs? Would you ensure that all testing organization have adequate resources to accomplish their missions?

Weapon system testing is necessary to ensure a developed system meets the warfighter's requirements prior to deployment. If confirmed, I will work with the Military Departments, the Chairman of the Joint Chiefs of Staff, and the Department's acquisition professionals to ensure that the department's acquisition system balances the need for adequate testing with the urgency to field our systems in a timely and cost-effective manner, and that the testing organizations have the resources required to accomplish their missions.

A natural tension exists between major program objectives to reduce cost and schedule and the T&E objective to ensure performance meets specifications and requirements.

What is your assessment of the appropriate balance between the desire to reduce acquisition cycle times and the need to perform adequate testing?

If confirmed, I will examine the risks associated with shortening test cycles and consult with the Service Chiefs and the Department's acquisition and testing professionals. It is my view that there must be an appropriate balance between reducing costs and cycle times while prudently ensuring that a system's performance meets requirements.

Under what circumstances, if any, do you believe we should procure weapon systems and equipment that has not been demonstrated through test and evaluation to be operationally effective, suitable, and survivable?

I support ensuring weapon systems are verified as operationally suitable before proceeding to high-rate production. Only in extraordinary, highly urgent circumstances should exceptions be considered.

Congress established the position of Director of Operational Test and Evaluation to serve as an independent voice on matters relating to operational testing of weapons systems. As established, the Director has a unique and direct relationship with Congress, consistent with the statutory independence of the office.

Do you support the continued ability of the Director of Operational Test and Evaluation's to speak freely and independently with the Congress?

Yes.

Funding for Science and Technology (S&T) Investments

What specific technological areas should the Defense Department prioritize for investment in order to develop next generation operational capabilities?

This is a critical question, and I owe it to the Committee and the President-elect to examine this issue carefully, if I am confirmed. In general, those areas identified in the development of the Third Offset strategy are worthy of investment. Further, we should seek a maximum return on investments in capabilities that ensure we retain our technological advantage.

What would you do to increase the interaction between the labs and the private sector? Similarly, how would you ensure that a greater percentage of the technologies being developed by the labs make it across the so-called "valley of death" and transition into programs of record and are deployed to the warfighter?

If confirmed, I will seek new options for simplifying and improving the success rate of putting new technologies into production, and I will seek the guidance of the Committee in this effort.

What would be your plans for the Third Offset strategy? Which areas would you emphasize and how would you ensure that these new technologies are developed and deployed quickly?

If confirmed, I will review the current portfolio of technologies under development and ensure that those provide the nation with long-term technological superiority. Once in office I would be able to give more detailed information to the Committee on my concrete priorities. In principle, I believe we should be tolerant of risk in order to foster innovation and encourage technological leaps.

Acquisition Reform and Innovation

How do you view the current state of the defense acquisition system and what changes do you want to see made to enable the system to better support innovation for the warfighter?

Poor acquisition outcomes are forfeiting U.S. technology advantages and depriving the nation of strategic capabilities. The fundamental challenge for the defense acquisition system is to deliver integrated hardware and software platforms that change on a routine basis. The government has a strong incentive to encourage the rapid adoption of existing and emerging technologies.

I will seek to establish a culture of innovation across the Department. A reformed system must ensure the government develops only capabilities designed to meet unique needs within the Services and Department of Defense organizations. If confirmed, I will work with the Congress, the Department's leadership, our acquisition and requirements professionals, and leaders within industry to provide capabilities to warfighters on an accelerated basis.

Acquisition Accountability

In your view, what role should the services and Service Chiefs have in delivering acquisition programs on time and on budget and who should be responsibility for large-scale acquisition failures? If confirmed, how would you improve acquisition accountability?

I believe that the process could be improved if Service Chiefs had increased responsibility and accountability for the successful development and fielding of large-scale acquisitions. If confirmed I will work to ensure that the Department of Defense recruits the best technical and program management talent available, gives those leaders the tools and authorities required for success, and holds them accountable for the successful execution of their program.

Reset and Reconstitution Funding

The Department has a substantial backlog of maintenance availabilities due to the high tempo and demand of more than a decade of combat operations. Senior DOD officials have testified that they will require 2-3 years of additional funding to restore readiness through reset and reconstitution of their equipment and personnel.

Do you agree with the assessment that the DOD will need 2-3 years of additional funding for reset and reconstitution?

Yes. We have not adequately funded the reset of the force after 15 years of hard use. If confirmed I will be in a better position to address the details of what it will really take to properly reset the force, as well as what the associated timeline is likely to be.

If confirmed, how will you balance maintenance and reset requirements with fiscal realities and future risk in developing your budget request?

If confirmed, I will seek to strike an appropriate balance in the budget request between the current and future requirements of the force. To do this well, I will need to rely on the insight and experience of this Committee.

Operational Energy

During your time in Iraq, you called on the Department to "unleash us from the tether of fuel."

What exactly did you mean and what experiences led to that comment?

I meant that units would be faced with unacceptable limitations because of their dependence on fuel, and that I wanted to be able to push those limits further. Meanwhile, our efforts to resupply the force with fuel made us vulnerable in ways that were exploited by the enemy.

Do you believe this issue remains a challenge for the Department of Defense?

Yes.

If confirmed, what will you do to unleash the Department from the tether of fuel?

The Department's acquisition process should explore alternate and renewable energy sources that are reliable, cost effective, and can relieve the dependence of deployed forces on vulnerable fuel supply chains to better enable our primary mission to win in conflict. The purpose of such efforts should be to increase the readiness and reach of our forces.

If confirmed, what priorities would you establish for Defense investments in and deployment of operational energy technologies to increase the combat capabilities of warfighters, reduce logistical burdens, and enhance mission assurance on our installations?

Investments in energy technologies should be prioritized according to the same standard as any other Department decision to invest in basic research and technology development, namely: their direct contribution to achieve the Department's primary missions; potential return on investment; protection of US national security interests; and contribution to enhancing readiness and combat effectiveness while reducing the vulnerability of our service members in battle. We should also take full advantage of private sector innovations that can provide military advantages.

Environment

If confirmed, will you comply with environmental regulations, laws and guidance from the Environmental Protection Agency?

Yes. Every year, the Department of Defense invests in critical environmental research and development to improve its environmental performance, reduce costs, and enhance and sustain mission capabilities.

If confirmed, will you make the same level of investment for DOD's Environmental Research Programs?

I am aware that every year, the Department of Defense works to improve the military's environmental performance, reduce costs, and enhance and sustain mission capabilities. If confirmed, I will review this issue with the guidance of the committee.

If confirmed, will you work with the Department of Interior and the U.S. Fish & Wildlife Service to find cooperative ways to ensure military readiness and protect the environment on and around U.S. military installations?

Yes. If confirmed, I will work with all departments and agencies of the federal government.

Congressional Oversight

In order to exercise its legislative and oversight responsibilities, it is important that this Committee and other appropriate committees of the Congress are able to receive testimony, briefings, and other communications of information.

Do you agree, if confirmed for this high position, to appear before this Committee and other appropriate committees of the Congress?

Yes.

Do you agree, if confirmed, to appear before this Committee, or designated members of this Committee, and provide information, subject to appropriate and necessary security protection, with respect to your responsibilities as Secretary of Defense?

Yes.

Do you agree to ensure that testimony, briefings and other communications of information are provided to this Committee and its staff and other appropriate Committees?

Yes.

Do you agree to provide documents, including copies of electronic forms of communication, in a timely manner when requested by a duly constituted Committee, or to consult with the Committee regarding the basis for any good faith delay or denial in providing such documents?

Yes.